Don Juan in Soho

Patrick Marber was born in 1964. He lives in London with his wife and their three sons.

PATRICK MARBER

Don Juan in Soho

after Molière

FABER & FABER

First published in 2007
by Faber and Faber Ltd
74–77 Great Russell Street
London WC1B 3DA

This edition, revised and reset, 2017

Typeset by Country Setting, Kingsdown, Kent CT14 8ES
Printed in England by CPI Group (UK) Ltd, Croydon CR0 4YY

A CIP record for this book is available from the British Library

978-0-571-33943-3

4 6 8 10 9 7 5 3

For Sidney

This play text went to press while rehearsals were still in progress, and may differ slightly from the play in performance.

Introduction

I wrote *Don Juan in Soho* in the summer of 2006. I hadn't written a full-length play for six years and this one was a great pleasure (and relief) to write. Simon Scardifield provided an excellent literal translation of the Molière original from which I worked. Simon also suggested the line, 'a true poet of the flesh', which Elvira uses in Act Four. My enduring thanks to him. Rhys Ifans agreed to play the leading role before I'd written a word – a truly inspiring leap of faith. I will always be indebted to him. The original cast and creative team delivered the play beautifully. The director was Michael Grandage: he commissioned the play, he helped me write it and he directed a terrific production of it. We had a lot of fun and I remember those days with huge affection for all involved.

Ten years later my wife was at a party and happened to be chatting to our old friend David Tennant. He mentioned that he was keen to do a play in 2017. So I sent him this one. A week later he phoned and said he'd be delighted to do it. Such luck is rare in the theatre and I thank my lucky stars for it. I had always wanted the play to have more life and this was the perfect opportunity for it to reach a wider audience with another sensational actor playing the title role.

I looked at the play again and made a few changes; I updated a few things, rewrote and trimmed it here and there but essentially it has the same spirit as the original, written in what now seems an innocent summer long ago.

PM, February 2017

Don Juan in Soho was first presented at the Donmar Warehouse, London, on 30 November 2006. The cast was as follows:

Colm Richard Flood
Stan Stephen Wight
DJ Rhys Ifans
Elvira Laura Pyper
Pete / Vagabond Abdul Salis
Lottie / Ruby Seroca Davis
Mattie / Dalia Jessica Brooks
Aloysius Chris Corrigan
Statue Tim Eagle
Louis David Ryall

Director Michael Grandage
Designer Christopher Oram
Lighting Designer Neil Austin
Composer and Sound Designer Adam Cork

Don Juan in Soho was first presented in this revised version at the Wyndham's Theatre, London on 17 March 2017 by Robert Fox for Robert Fox Ltd, Matthew Byam Shaw, Nia Janis and Nick Salmon for Playful Productions in association with Sonia Friedman Productions. The cast was as follows:

Col David Jonsson
Stan Adrian Scarborough
DJ David Tennant
Elvira Danielle Vitalis
Adam William Spray
Pete Theo Barklem-Biggs
Lottie Dominique Moore
Mattie / Ruby Alice Orr-Ewing
Vagabond Himesh Patel
Statue Mark Extance / Adrian Richards
Aloysius Mark Ebulué
Dalia Eleanor Wyld
Kristal Emma Naomi
Louis Gawn Grainger

Director Patrick Marber
Set and Costume Designer Anna Fleischle
Lighting Designer Mark Henderson
Composer and Sound Designer Adam Cork
Video Designer Dick Straker
Movement Polly Bennett
Casting Director Robert Sterne CDG
Company Stage Manager Claire Sibley
Deputy Stage Manager Nina Scholar
Assistant Stage Manager Christopher Carr
Associate Director Audrey Sheffield

Characters

in order of speaking

Col

Stan

DJ

Elvira

Adam

Pete

Lottie

Mattie

Vagabond

Aloysius

Statue

Dalia

Ruby

Louis

Kristal

The play is set in London in the near present

DON JUAN IN SOHO

Act One

A statue of King Charles II alone on stage.

Music. Mozart's 'Don Giovanni' overture or something modern. Or both.

The company perform a strange, sensual dance. It can be eerie. And a bit comical. But not too long.

They set the stage. Then clear it. Leaving:

Afternoon.

The large open-plan lobby of a swank, modern hotel in Soho.

Stan (still young enough to have hope, rumpled, not tall) sits with a bottle of beer and a neat double scotch. Also a small jar of cashew nuts.

Col (late twenties, earnest, noble) enters and sees Stan.

Col WHERE IS HE?!

Stan I'm sorry?

Col Is he here? He *must* be here!

Stan Well he's not!

Col senses a lie. His eyes wander to the jar of nuts . . .

Col Are they from a mini-bar? Did you stay here last night?

Stan Nahhh. There's a little nut man on Berwick Street. Chinese bloke. I love a nut. Want one?

Col Where were you last night?

Stan I was tucked up in bed!

Col *Where?*

Stan In my lowly hovel!

Col So where's *he*?

Stan I don't know!

Col Then what are you doing here?

Stan Can't a man have an innocent beer without being molested?

Col (*points to other drink*) Who's this for? *He* drinks scotch.

Stan It's for *me*, it's a chaser!

Col So neither of you stayed here last night?

Stan Why would he stay here when he's got a lovely new wife to go home to?

Col I don't know! But Elvira's in pieces. We've called the police, the hospitals and I've searched every hotel in town. He's *vanished*! Our only concern is his safety, if he's here then *please*, *tell me*.

Stan I would if I could but he's not so I can't.

Col (*suddenly*) Your nuts are from the mini-bar of a room in this hotel!

He tries to snatch the nuts. After a brief struggle he grabs the jar and prods the logo vigorously.

There! There! The logo! I ask you once more, in the name of God, IS HE HERE?

Stan (*aside*) Can I betray the man who has clothed and fed me these two decades? (*To Col.*) He's in the penthouse suite.

Col Thank you! Wha— what's he doing there?

Stan He's banging a Croatian supermodel.

Col emits a small scream.

You did ask.

Col Has he gone mad? He's a married man! My sister is a person of purity, of quality – she's a *colossal* human being. She was a virgin.

Stan Well, we all were.

Col (*testily*) I mean on her wedding day. A Croatian supermodel – this is a terrible shock.

Stan I know, he usually favours a bit of Bosnian.

Col There have been *other* episodes?

Stan Well, it's possible – but don't quote me.

Col But – but he seems so *charming*, and so in *love*, how can this *be*?

Stan Oh, the modern monster *conceals* himself. Don't expect a fiend to be fanged. Ever seen a dictator with blood on his hands? *Never!* First the manicure, then the massacre.

Col And – and – he's fornicating with this lady as we speak?

Stan Making shapes like balloon animals. He texted me a pic of the hotel and one word, 'Noon'. I waited an hour, nothing, so up I go. Knock knock. He opens the door, stark testicle naked and full morning glory. She's on all fours, nude as a spoon. I recognised her immediately.

Col How?

Stan She's *famous* – she's on the circuit. (*Remembering, transfixed.*) So there she is: all sloe-eyed and luscious . . . full Brazilian . . . she's *glistening*. Gives me a friendly wink with her arse'ole – which *I* think is a bit forward.

Col That's enough information.

Stan He goes, 'Be a good chap and wait downstairs.' I scored the nuts and two hours later here we are. I 'spect he'll be down soon. Or not. I once waited three days for him in the lobby of the Bangkok Sheraton. Go on, treat yourself, have a cashew.

Col is still in shock. He hands the jar back to Stan.

Stan You see, what you're dealing with here is a savage, he's a *pirate*. Forgive my lack of discretion, but the man's a *slag*. He'd do it with anything – a hole in the ozone layer. All he lives for is chasing skirt and once in a blue moon, trouser. And it's not just models and virgins, oh no, he's *seedy* – likes a bit of rough to vary the menu; endless nights have I chauffered him to the reeking slums as he preys on the deranged and the destitute: the pickled, raging prozzer on parole, the sweetly simpering smackhead, the near corpse of an ancient hag dinkled with filth – he's not choosy! Apart from a brief hiatus last winter he's had, on average, three different women a day for a quarter of a century – you do the maths. You might say – *he* does – what's wrong with a young(*ish*) man getting his rocks off on a very regular basis? Well I'll tell you: the rocks create an avalanche of *agony* – he's a cheating, betraying, lying dog and I've wasted the best years of my life mopping up after him. Well, I've had enough of his broody Byronic bullshit. He's had every privilege known to man and pissed it up a wall – as a point of principle! NOT THAT HE'S GOT ANY!

Col What happened last winter?

Stan Syphilis. (*Wistfully.*) 'Love' – 'loyalty' – 'truth', all that you and I hold dear he craps on. He's Satan in a suit from Savile Row, no exaggeration, he's a *terrorist*. Your new brother-in-law has declared jihad against the human spirit. And he's made me *cynical*. I hate him, I hate him,

I – Hate – Him! (*Beat.*) I've never said that before – this is progress! (*Beat.*) You see, he hurts people, enjoys it – *seeks* it. It's all sport to him. And now he's done it to your sister, the most innocent of them all. It makes me heave, it's so unfair. I wish he'd just . . . (*Darkly.*) I wish there was a hell he could burn in forever.

Col There is a hell.

Stan Oh, don't give me hope.

Col Hell is real.

Col whips out his mobile.

Stan Ooh, I wouldn't tell her!

Col I am compelled to!

Stan By who??

Col By all that is decent and right! Have you no moral code?

Stan Of course I have, it's just hard to decipher it when he's around!

Col dials.

Don't tell her – I shouldn't have told you – I'll get the blame now!

Col How can you associate with this reptile? Aren't you ashamed of yourself?

Stan Yes!

Col THEN SHOW IT, MAN! You're a disgrace, you fester just like him!

Stan Hey, there's no need for that, I'm on *your* side!

Col Maggot! Every part of you is corrupted, you're a moral black hole!

He puts the phone back in his pocket, can't get through.

Oh, the wrath of my family will be fearsome. You've met my stepbrother?

Stan (*aside, scared*) He refers to Vicious Aloysius.

Col He will exact his revenge on *both* of you. No mercy. Especially not for his – *ligger.*

Stan (*angrily*) I am NOT a ligger, I am a *paid* employee!

Col You're just a dogsbody!

Stan *No*, I am paid to enable and – and facilitate his lifestyle. I am the keeper of the database (*Holds iPhone aloft.*) I've got twenty thousand numbers in here!

Col You're nothing but a fly on a horse's shitey arse! I and my brother will be the tail that smites the fly. And the horse too!

Stan Oh, be gone – and take your terrible metaphors with you!

Col (*exiting*) I'm coming back!

Stan calls after him.

Stan I'll deny everything! You've no proof!

Stan paces a moment, worried. Enter DJ, immaculate in a bespoke suit.

DJ Did you pine for me while I was gone? Oh you *did*, you darling little munchkin.

Stan glances nervously at the exit. DJ sees this and looks too.

Was that my brother-in-law?

Stan Where?

DJ Exiting.

Stan I think it might've been.

DJ Well, *was* it? Don't lie, you're a feeble dissembler.

Stan It was him.

DJ ponders a moment.

DJ You covered for me?

Stan As ever.

DJ (*doubtfully*) Hmm. (*Sits.*) Furnish me, please.

Stan You can't smoke here.

DJ Watch me.

DJ beckons Stan to give him a cigarette. Stan sticks one in DJ's mouth and lights it. DJ inhales. He reaches for his scotch, but it's a tiny bit out of reach. He could stretch and reach it but chooses not to. He makes a feeble groan of incapability. He gestures to Stan, who pushes the glass a precise two inches towards him. DJ groans again. Finally, Stan puts the glass in his hand.

God bless you.

DJ luxuriates a moment, content. Stan hovers, tense.

Stan We might want to skedaddle fairly soon. I think Elvira's on her way. Despite my guile it's possible the brother inferred a certain 'furtivity' in the building.

DJ Stan, you seem flustered.

Stan Well, actually, I've been doing some quite serious thinking.

DJ (*mock-concerned*) Ohhh. Well, *oooh*. You're perfectly free to resign.

Stan How could I when the money's so good?

DJ I've told you, you will have your wages.

Stan Yeah but *when?*

DJ Oh, don't be so mercenary. You don't need wages, your *perks* are more than generous: sole use of the Jag, extensive travel, the odd line of dampening coke from the cistern, an occasional fumble with my devastated rejects, hmm? A wiser man would regard my tutelage as payment in itself. There's an art to seduction and (forgive me) a fellow who is no oil painting might prosper more by whingeing *less* and learning from the master.

Stan bristles with frustration, then takes out his iPhone.

Stan (*nods upstairs*) So shall I bung her details on the database?

DJ I've told you not to use that word, you vulgarise the beautiful.

Stan Do you want her filed on the *aide-mémoire?*

DJ thinks, weighing up the possibility of seeing her again.

DJ If you must.

Stan Category?

DJ 'C'.

Stan Huh. Thought she'd be a 'B'. Live and learn.

He sighs and starts tapping away.

Stan 'Name' . . . 'place of assignation' . . . and, any hobbies?

DJ She enjoys badminton.

Stan Ooh, can't beat a bit of badders. (*Finishes tapping.*) The lady is logged.

DJ I know you worship your 'database' but I want you to abandon it. I accept that it's human to 'organise', and the world will insist on its lazy distinctions, but they are ugly and inexact: rich/poor, homo/hetero, male/female, black/white, good/bad. (*Beat.*) The only useful distinction is that between the 'fuckable' and the 'unfuckable'.

Stan You what?

DJ In the end, it's all that counts.

Stan So . . . what am I?

DJ Put it this way, the fuckable tend to *know* they are. We might for our amusement admit a second category of distinction . . .

Stan (*hopefully*) We might?

DJ Between the 'haveable' and the 'unhaveable'.

Stan Good, what am I?

DJ Oh, 'haveable'.

Stan Excellent!

DJ Actually, it's better to be 'unhaveable'.

Stan Oh.

DJ Think about it; the truly desirable are both 'fuckable' *and* 'unhaveable'.

Stan Hang on, *you're* haveable, you're haveable just like me!

DJ Yes but I'm also magnificently fuckable, the rule thus proven by my exception. But don't dwell on it, you're only a troll – a mere atom in the carnal firmament – and as I say, these distinctions are all terribly dubious.

Stan stuffs his iPhone back in his pocket. DJ exhales, thinks, drinks, smokes then twitches a touch, in pain.

DJ I'm feeling the twinge.

Stan But you've just been – (*Gestures upstairs.*) All night!

DJ That was the past, where's the next one?

Stan Don't look at *me*, I'm an unfuckable troll.

DJ (*muses*) I've never done it with an Eskimo. I'd like a furry little Eskimo lady. Book a flight to Alaska, hire appropriate kit and a pack of huskies. I'll be shouting 'mush' by the end of the week.

Stan I'm on it.

DJ I *mean* it.

Stan I know you mean it, I mean it too.

DJ Stan, you're a prude. It's getting on my titties. Why this simmering *disapproval*? There's no inherent virtue in monogamy, why make a fetish of fidelity – it's *unnatural*. Praise the priapic, not the parsimonious! Down with selfishness and up with *me* – a dippy old hippy who's generous with his *lurve*. Yes, I've a penchant for the perverse but who doesn't, in their dreams? All I seek is pleasure in all its rich and various forms – where's the *harm*? I'm not a rapist, I don't fiddle with children, well, not since I *was* one. I'm a radical feminist, I'm not a snob (witness *your* presence), I don't litter, I'm *very* nice to animals and I'm certainly not a racist: the pungent Persian, the Nip nymphette, the jiggling Jewess, the babe in the burka, the moustachioed lady of the Ukraine, the big, boogie-woogie mamma – all are *lovely* to my gaze. I'm not a baddie, I'm good news! I'm on a humanitarian mission: I'm the Gandhi of the gang bang, the Bishop Desmond Tutu of titillation, the Dalai Lama of desire – what's not to love? I'm the Martin Luther King of copulation!

Stan So what about Elvira? She's been *harmed*, she'll be destroyed!

DJ We live in a world where collateral damage is inevitable. But we must not be deterred from our chosen path.

Stan Can we please pay the bill and get going?

DJ (*gestures to reception*) Off you pop.

Stan (*waves his credit card*) I'm building up a very, very heavy debt here, I'd really appreciate some *funds*.

DJ gives him a vague dismissive wave of the hand. A recurrent gesture.
   Stan moves towards the reception desk. Stops. Warns the audience.

Stan (*aside*) *Please* don't be charmed, he's not a loveable rogue. He really *isn't*.

Enter Elvira with Col following behind. Elvira is in her early twenties, delightful, distraught.

Oh, Lord.

He scuttles off to the reception desk.

Elvira Is it true?

DJ stares at her, distantly.

'I'm just going out for a packet of fags.' That was twenty-four hours ago.

DJ raises his packet of cigarettes.

And you've been here with this . . . ?

Col (*sotto, mortified*) Croatian supermodel.

Elvira Well? (*Pause.*) *Well?*

DJ Me? Oh, yes. Yes, I am that trouper.

Elvira We got back from our honeymoon *yesterday*. We've been married a *fortnight*. You made a vow before God.

DJ Ah. Not known at this address.

Elvira comes over to DJ. She strokes his face, tenderly.

Elvira Are – are you having a panic attack about getting married?

DJ No! Lord, no. I hugely enjoyed our marriage.

Silence. Elvira absorbs the information.

Elvira So – so – do you want to – to separate? Or to – to . . . divorce?

DJ Why not?

Elvira Well *which*?

DJ It's all much of a muchness.

Elvira No it's not! What do you want, damn you?

DJ I want to drink my drink and fuck an Eskimo.

Pause.

Elvira Wh— what *are* you?

DJ Oh, just a cunt with an eye for one.

Stan (*aside*) You see, I told you!

Elvira Did you ever love me?

DJ stares at her.

But you pursued me to the bleakest places on earth – Darfur, Calais, Syria – wherever I was working. You donated truckfuls of aid, you lived in a tent, starved in the desert. You wept an ocean, threatened suicide – and the *poetry*, a whole sequence of sonnets. You marched against landmines, ran marathons for Oxfam, sang lullabies to orphaned children. You did yoga!

DJ Well, you were an *awfully* tough nut to crack. But I'm afraid your relentless do-gooding has done my head in. You live in a world of quinoa and almond milk latte, it's just not my cup of tea. Present circumstance has alerted me to the most frightening word in the dictionary – it's *wife*. Though *commedia dell'arte* comes a close second. (*Jauntily.*) Sorry it hurts but these things do.

Elvira (*realising*) On our honeymoon . . . when you went for your morning stroll along the beach . . . ?

DJ (*confirming her suspicion*) Elevenses.

Elvira And your second 'stroll' before dinner?

DJ Aperitif.

Elvira And – on . . . our wedding day . . . ?

DJ Your mother's rather striking sister.

Col (*horrified*) Auntie Laura?!

DJ She was weeping with joy, we hugged, there was a stirring. And then . . . a *recognition*. We rutted like jackals on a mossy grave.

Elvira WHY DID YOU MARRY ME?

DJ I need a wee. Stan, be a good sport and tell her?

He exits. Elvira crumples. Col comforts her. Her pain is terrible.

Elvira (*to Stan*) Tell me . . .

Stan Erm – well – love – *life* . . . it's all very confusing, isn't it?

Elvira No, it's very simple. We're here to love each other and to change the world for good.

Stan *Yes!* I agree! And I'm sure he . . . Oh, God.

Col Tell her, so she can grieve.

Stan (*quickly*) He married you so you'd sleep with him.

Silence.

Elvira No other reason?

Stan None. He's pure in that respect.

Elvira But there are *millions* of women in the world to sleep with. Why do this to *me*?

Stan You were innocent – and there's not a lot of that about. And you're noble and lovely – and, oh, it's just horribly bad luck, but it's really not personal.

Elvira He's my *husband*. Till death. I can't 'unlove' him. (*Hopefully.*) Maybe if . . . if I *spoke* to him . . . if . . . he knew how much he is *loved* . . .?

Stan Oh, he doesn't want to be loved.

Col He is *gone*! He is Lucifer and there's an end to it. We will go home and we will gather the family.

Stan (*aside, nervously*) Gather the family?

Col puts his arms round Elvira. Both are close to tears.

Col It was all an elaborate pose, a diabolical strategy for seduction. He campaigned for two years simply to – to ravish you a fortnight.

Elvira And his cruelty is unforgivable. But oh, *what* ravishment it was!

Col No! Don't glorify the beast!

Elvira You don't understand, he has *perverted* me, *defiled* me, spun me from fear to ferocity!

Col Banish the memory!

Elvira He took me every which way and other ways so fiendish I knew not my way out of! It was an *explosion* –

he unleashed me! He would torture me and I him, both of us begging for more!

Col Enough!

Elvira Oh – the sinful, filthy fantasies he drew out of me! What I would do, what I would have him watch me do! I have never known that such things could be done and said and be so magnificent! (*Pause.*) And now *this* – his terrible disdain – a punishment for my debauchery. (*Pause.*) He has used me, broken me . . . and now spurns me as a spoilt child discards a once-favoured toy, so – so casually, so brutally . . . oh, I am not like this. I am strong but he has obliterated me.

   She exits.

Col We will mince him in the courts. We will shame his name to the world. We will have our *justice*!

   He exits. Stan reflects, ashamed. DJ appears, sprightly.

DJ Spot of good, good news at this upsetting time. While I was in the gents this young rugger-bugger bounces in and scores three packets of Durex from the machine. He's *aglow*, he's actually bloody *singing*. (*Sings 'I'm getting married in the morning'.*) I say, '*Are* you?' He says, 'Well, no, actually, I've just *got* married this afternoon and we're having our wedding party tonight on a boat going down the Thames. We wanted to do something really special.' 'Congrats!' I say. 'Bloody well done and good luck to you.' He says, 'Oh, I've *had* all the luck *I* deserve. My wife is the most gorgeous woman you could ever meet.' (*Pause.*) 'Well, can I meet her?' He says, 'Yes, she's waiting out there.' We emerge from the gents and standing there is – this – *fox*. She says, 'Oh, I missed you, darling.' *I* say, (*Noël Coward.*) 'Did you, did you really?' We – All – Laugh. I proffer more congrats, 'Well done, well *done* –'

At this moment the happy couple pass through the lobby, arm in arm, in their wedding attire. DJ waves to them.

DJ I say, do enjoy your cruise down the river!

The man (Adam) waves back as they exit.

Adam Ahoy there!

DJ turns to Stan.

DJ Now, we're going to need a motor boat.

Stan presses his forehead in pain as they exit.

Act Two

Late night.
   A hospital. Accident and Emergency department,
waiting area.
   Strip lighting, rows of chairs. Various injured or ill
patients waiting to be seen.
   Stan sits, shivering, a hospital blanket around his
shoulders. He is sopping wet. Pete (also soaked) sits with
him, waiting.
   Lottie enters with a holdall full of clothes. She comes
bustling over to Pete.

Pete Oh, cheers, love!

Lottie Oh yeah, no *problem*! I was only snoozin' on the
sofa, all mellowed out from a spliff an' a few Stellas.

   Pete tries to kiss her, she recoils.

Wot u all wet for? You ming like an old toilet!

Pete Was it on the news?

Lottie I don't do the news, it's depressin'.

Pete There's been a boat accident!

Lottie Yeah, *and*?

Pete I was *there*, I saw it happen!

Lottie Yeahan*so*?

Pete There's been casualties! *He's* one of 'em. (*Points to
Stan.*) I fished 'im out the Thames!

Lottie Wot, u went in the river?

Pete Yeah!

Lottie Wot was you doin' on a boat?

Pete I wasn't on the boat, I was walking Moses!

Lottie STUPID FUCKIN' DOG!

Pete An I 'eard this big bang. It's dark so I can't see too much but this motor boat's got outta control, it's gone steamin' into this other bigger boat where there's this party goin' on, music an' that.

Lottie Shouldn't 'ave a party on a boat! (*Points to Stan.*) So who's 'e?

Pete I dunno, some bloke!

Lottie *So?*

Pete So I elped 'im din' I? I saved 'is life!

Lottie Wot d'you want, an OBE?!

Pete 'Im an 'is mate were in the river an' I went in an' 'elped 'em ashore!

Lottie 'Ashore'? Whassat?

Pete THE SHORE!! (*Pause, explains.*) The bit of *land* next to the river!

    Pause.

Lottie Reckon you might get a reward? Could be a few quid in it.

Pete I didn't do it to get a reward!

Lottie Yeah, but if there *is*, if there's one *goin'*, be stupid not to, all I'm sayin'.

Pete Well there ain't.

Lottie How dya know?

Pete I don't know but there ain't – I ain't askin' for one.

Lottie (*furiously*) Well, thas why you're a pauper cos you don't see the *angle*! Loadsa wealfy arse'oles all twatting it up on a boat an' you come along like fuckin' Batman an' you don't reckon one of 'em might slip you a fuckin' *fiver*?!

Pause.

Pete I s'pose I could mention it . . .

Lottie Course you could!

Pete (*points to Stan*) He did say his mate's an Earl . . .

Lottie (*excitedly*) Wot, like a Lord?

Pete No! An *Earl* – an actual Earl of – the realm. Earls are better, less of 'em. 'Cept he's not one yet, his dad's one and he's gonna be.

Lottie Well, he's got a few quid is the point.

Pete Yeah, maybe.

Lottie 'Maybe' my *vulva*! He's an Earl, he's got a few quid, OK?

Pete OK.

Lottie So where is 'e?

Pete In with the doctor.

Lottie (*panicking*) 'E's not gonna die on us, is 'e?

Pete Nahh, 'e's *fine*. This one's a bit poorly but the Earl got seen first. Jumped the queue. I s'pose there's a – a protocol.

Lottie 'Ave to be.

Pause.

Pete Since you ask, *I'm* alright. I didn't drown or get pneumonia, since you ask, thanks for your concern.

Lottie Oh, thass right, give it the big 'I am', won't ya? I can see *you're* alright cos you're standin' 'ere like the big purple bellend you always is!

Pause.

Pete Lot?

Lottie Wot?

Pete Do you actually love me?

Lottie Course I do!

Pete No, cos, if some stranger was to 'ear you they might think you don't cos of the way you talk to me.

Lottie Wot way? Wot you sayin'?

Pete I nearly died and i's like you don't care.

Lottie Course I care, course I care – you sayin' I'm a bitch?

Pete No!

Lottie 'Ere, come 'ere.

Gives Pete a cuddle.

You're my 'ero, OK?

Pete Yeah.

She goes over to Stan, who almost shrinks in fear. Meanwhile Pete sorts through the bag of clothes selecting items for himself, Stan and DJ.

Lottie Alright, mate. You a bit sodden?

Stan Mmm.

Lottie Ahh. So your mate, is he royal or sumfink?

Stan He's from a very old English family.

Lottie He live in a castle an' that?

Stan A very large estate.

Lottie Yeah, me too. Wot sort?

Stan Well, farmland and a huge lake, stables, paddocks, orchards, fields, villages . . .

Lottie (*to Pete*) Are you *listening*?! (*To Stan.*) An' what, it's all old and shit?

Stan Parts of the estate date back to the fourteenth century.

Lottie I prefer modern. So – what – you 'is butler?

Stan And chauffeur.

Lottie I'd fuckin' love a chauffeur! 'Scuse my langwidge. D'you wear a peaked 'at an' double buttons on a sorta tunicky fing?

Stan When he tells me to.

Lottie How d'you become that then?

Stan Oh, my family have worked for his for centuries. When I left school I thought I might – well, I didn't quite know *what* to do.

Lottie Chase, cut to.

Stan I fell into it.

Pete hands Stan some garments.

Pete 'Ere you go, mate.

Lottie Summa Pete's shitty gear but it's better than a blanket, innit?

Stan Thank you.

Stan sneezes.

Pete Bless you. You wanna come to the gents, get changed?

Stan I don't want to miss my place, I – I really do *need* to see a doctor.

Lottie You go, Pete, we'll wait 'ere.

Pete You sure?

Lottie Yeah. (I'm doin' *bizness.*)

Pete exits. Lottie cosies up to Stan. She holds the blanket round him so he can change into a new top.

So . . . this *Earl*, is he like one of them kindly, aristocratic gentlemen with whiskers or is he a well-miserly bastard? Cos I'm not saying nuthink but Pete (who is my boyfriend) did save his life. I mean, it's gotta be worth a few grand, innit? A man's life. An' yours an' all . . .

Stan Oh, I don't have any money on me, it was in my wallet and it's all ruined.

Lottie (*punches him amiably*) I don't mean *now*! I mean . . . 'in due course'. (*Firmly.*) So you'll 'ave a word with the Earl?

Stan As soon as he returns.

Lottie Wanna get me tits done.

Stan I'm sorry?

Lottie Need the money to go up 'Arley Street. Do me tits. See.

She demonstrates the look she'd like, raising her bosom and clasping her breasts together.

DJ Don't you dare change a *thing.*

Lottie turns. DJ stands watching her, has been there a while, unseen. He wears a white coat and trousers stolen from the hospital. He could almost be a doctor.

Please remain perfectly still.

He walks round her, slowly, observing her parts.

Lottie Are you a doctor?

DJ I'm a specialist. May I? Please?

She presents her breasts. A little nervously. He has a good long feel. Lottie has not been touched so gently and carefully for years. She stares at him, intensely. And he her.

Lottie Are you allowed to be touching me like this?

DJ I'm not touching you. I'm examining you.

Lottie Have I passed?

DJ Oh, yes. These are exquisite. Please. Don't succumb to the knife.

Lottie (*purring with pleasure*) Keep it real?

DJ (*softly*) Keep it really real.

His hands stray down to her crotch and her behind. Stan can barely believe it.

Lottie I know what you're doing.

DJ I know you know. But when faced with such pulchritude what's a poor medic to do? Will you show me your teeth? (*She does.*) And now just tickle your front two teeth with the tip of your charming tongue. (*She does.*) Splendid. And if I may touch your tongue with the very tip of mine? (*She lets him.*) Good. Really very good. You're quite the most perfect patient I've seen all day. I'd like to write an article about you. For *The Lancet*. Will you come to my surgery, *now*?

Lottie (*murmuring*) Where is it?

DJ Just . . . down that corridor.

He scoops her up in his arms. They're about to exit when Pete comes back in, doing up his tracksuit.

Pete Oi! Wot you doin'?!

Lottie I's alright, Pete, he's a *doctor*.

Pete No 'e ain't! 'E's the bloke, the *Earl*!

Lottie Eh?

Pete 'E's the bloke I got out the river!

Lottie (*still entwined with DJ*) Are you the Earl?

DJ You bet I am.

Pete approaches them but Stan (reluctantly but expertly) blocks his way.

Pete (*to Stan*) I saved 'is life an' now 'e's at it with my girlfriend!

Stan He's in shock.

Pete Lottie?

DJ (*to Stan*) Hold him back!

Pete tries to approach again but Stan holds him back.

Pete Let me go!

DJ (*to Lottie*) You're better than this. Be my wife, my love, my life. Share my wealth, own my heart, be my *Countess*.

Pete Lotters!

Stan (*to Pete*) Behave!

DJ (*to Lottie*) You are tender and sensual and in your own naughty way, you are *pure*.

Lottie Yes!

DJ And no one knows it!

Lottie No!

DJ They've never understood you!

Lottie It's true!

DJ I want to make love to you. Has anyone ever made *love* to you – Charlotte?

Lottie Carlotta.

Pete Lots! Help! Someone!

He breaks free from Stan, approaches menacingly, fists raised. DJ sees this and immediately affects a strange fit.

DJ I'm swooning . . . I swoon . . . (*Sotto, to Lottie.*) Catch me, darling.

He 'feints'. She catches him and in one sweeping romantic movement lays him down on the seats, cradling his head in her arms.

Pete Whassgoinon?

Lottie Go an' have a fag, you don't unnerstand.

Pete Eh?

Lottie Please, babes.

Pete But I love ya!

Lottie So gimme a moment. I gotta – I gotta be *alone*. *Please.*

Pete Moses is in the motor. I'm gonna give him a little walk round the block. An' then I'm comin' back an you're comin' wiv me!

Pete exits. Lottie strokes DJ. Her hand strays to his crotch. Expertly she takes a spare blanket and conceals her activities beneath it.

Lottie Oh, come back to life. Please. Oh . . . *here* you are.

DJ (*murmuring, innocently*) Oh . . . wh . . . wha . . . what's happening . . . ?

Lottie (*whispering*) I'm here . . . Lottie's here . . .

Lottie gently masturbates DJ.
Now, a lone woman (Mattie) walks through from the hospital and sits two seats down from DJ. She's still wearing her wedding dress but it's wet and dirty. She quietly breaks down. DJ's 'spider sense' starts to tingle. He opens one eye.

DJ (*to Stan, sotto*) Is that the *fox*?

Stan (*sighs*) Yes.

DJ What's she doing?

Stan She's crying.

DJ Bingo!

He thinks, comes up with a plan.

(*To Lottie.*) Oh . . . er . . . ah . . . darling, darling.

He stops Lottie's hand and whispers in her ear. She nods lasciviously. DJ sits up and surreptitiously lifts the blanket, Lottie ducks under it and starts to fellate DJ. Stan stares in wonderment and outrage. DJ catches his eye.

Heigh ho.

Lottie's head continues its discreet bob beneath the blanket.

Stan (*aside, of Mattie*) Her new husband is in a coma

DJ's right forefinger makes a slow, elegant move across the chairs between himself and the huddled, softly weeping Mattie.
He prepares a look of sincerity then taps her on the shoulder.

DJ Hi. (*Nods at the awfulness of it all.*) How is he?

Mattie Unconscious.

DJ (*pained sigh*) Oh.

Mattie They don't know whether he'll make it.

DJ He will! He has you to wake for. (*Stifles a gasp of pleasure.*) Hrrr!

Lottie's bobbing increases in speed. DJ rests his left elbow on her blanketed head subtly controlling her rhythm. She slows down.

Are your friends in with him?

Mattie nods.

You needed some space? (*Nods, sagely.*) It's almost impossible not to think of Percy Bysshe Shelley.

Mattie Didn't he drown?

DJ I meant the poetry, not the demise. Hrrr!

Mattie becomes vaguely conscious, despite her grief, that something is amiss in DJ's lap. Quick as a flash Stan passes DJ the holdall. DJ places it on the empty seat between himself and Mattie thus blocking her view of his lap. He nods insouciantly, then slowly shakes his head.

DJ Please forgive my innocent romantic gesture; to deliver a jeroboam to your boat, to celebrate your – (*Sudden gasp of pleasure.*) luhuhuhve.

Mattie Thank you. It was a lovely thought.

DJ One could not have predicted how choppy the black Thames might be this dread – (*Again.*) niiiiiihhhght.

Mattie Adam was very drunk . . . and *so* happy . . . but *why*, why did he jump in, why risk himself?

DJ Because that's the kind of beautiful, selfless guy he was!

Mattie *Is.*

DJ We met all too briefly but he had such spirit! (*As if perceiving an apparition.*) I can see him in the water – Ahoy! I tried to reach him but – oh – oh – oh –

> *A sudden pre-orgasmic rush of pleasure overcomes him. He disguises it with moans of misery for Adam.*

Oh – oh – oh, it's so – so – so – so – so – so – so *sad*. But we mustn't relive it – OH! – We *must not* go there.

> *DJ elbows Lottie into a much slower rhythm.*

We must be present only to 'now'.

Mattie Yes. What do you mean?

DJ Wouldn't Adam want us to live in the joyous, life-affirming manner in which *he* lived?

Mattie (*firmly*) He's not *dead*.

DJ His sense of adventure, his instinctive understanding of the present moment and the terrible contingency of things? (*Again.*) Hrrr! I want to comfort you tonight.

Mattie Comfort me?

DJ Adam can't. Tonight, I am him – for you.

Mattie What?

DJ Let's depart this deathly place and return to the hotel –

Mattie reacts.

– and *weep* and *mourn* and watch the sun rise, it will be our solace as we hold each other.

Mattie You want to *hold* me?

DJ If that's your request, then *yes*, I shall hold you all niiiiiiiiiinnnnniiiiiiiight.

Mattie stares at him, not sure what's happening. Another spasm of Lottie-induced pleasure takes hold of DJ. He disguises it again as a strange, yodelling serenade.

I will hohhoohohoohohohohhoohohohooooolllllllddd you.

Mattie I – I think you're in trauma. It can make one behave eccentrically. I know you were driving the motor boat but you mustn't blame yourself. It was an accident. The doctors are surprisingly good here, perhaps a sedative might help?

DJ (*sudden loud, deep moan of pleasure*) Whuuuurrrrr!

Mattie What?

DJ Flashback!

He curbs Lottie a bit.

Mattie Should I get a doctor?

DJ is nearing his climax.

DJ The dark, freezing water, oh – oh – ooh – horrorrrrr! (*Regains control a moment.*) Now, where were we? *Yes*, I want very much to hold you tonight.

Pause.

Mattie Are you *hitting* on me?!

DJ May I answer that question in *one* second?

He succumbs to the orgasm in his own peculiar and silent way. And now straight back into action:

(*To Mattie.*) Yes! I am hitting on you. In *Adam's* name.

Mattie You've got a fucking nerve!

DJ Nerve, cojones and a lovely, big cock.

Lottie pops her head out from under the blanket.

Lottie (*to DJ*) Alright, sailor?

Mattie (*realising*) Oh my God.

DJ (*to Lottie*) Good Lord, what are you doing there?

Mattie Oh my God.

Lottie Was it nice?

DJ (*to Lottie*) Sublime.

Mattie Oh my God.

Lottie (*to Stan*) What's 'sir blime'?

Stan (*to Lottie*) It means 'very nice'.

Lottie sits back proudly, barely conscious of the escalating situation.

Mattie YOU EVIL SHIT!

DJ It's a fair cop!

Mattie leaps up.

Mattie My husband is dying in there! *You* killed him! Sick fucking animal!

She goes for DJ, enraged, clawing at him.

Lottie Oi, leave off 'im!

She jumps up, ready for combat, pulls Mattie off.

Mattie (*to Lottie*) Do you know this man?

Lottie (*to Mattie*) Yeah, I'm the *Countess*!

Mattie He's a MURDERER!

Lottie Er – *no* – he's an Earl of the Realm!

Mattie He was trying to seduce me! He's a killer!

Lottie He's a specialist doctor!

Mattie Call the police!

Lottie She's asking for a smack!

Mattie POLICE!

Lottie Will someone fuckin' strangle her?!

Mattie POLICE!

Stan (*to DJ*) Exit?

DJ (*to Stan*) Pronto!

Mattie POLICE!

DJ and Stan prepare to slip away but Lottie grabs DJ.

Lottie I want you to make love to me, like you said, all slow and sirblime!

DJ I never said it would be slow!

Mattie Over here!

Stan sees hospital staff on their way.

Stan Has to be *now*!

Mattie (*pointing*) Here!

Lottie Don't you want to? You said you loved me!

DJ I might've overstated my position!

Mattie (*pointing*) Him! Him! Him!

Lottie Was it all shit about bein' your Countess?

DJ Total bollocks!

Lottie wails. Hospital staff arrive to sort out the mayhem.

Mattie This man is a criminal!

Lottie He stole my 'eart!

Mattie Arrest him at once!

Lottie Torture the wanker!

Staff try to grab DJ.

DJ Unhand me! I'm staff!

Pete (*entering*) Fuckin' dog's done a crap in the car!

Lottie (*desparately*) Pete! Save me! I got outta me depth!

Pete wades in, wildly hitting out as the skirmish increases. Other patients join in for the hell of it.

Mattie Arrest everyone!

Stan gets hit trying to free DJ. Mattie is now on the floor, wailing. Lottie clings to Pete, bawling her heart out. DJ finally extracts himself from the group, surveys the carnage with a delirious grin of pleasure.

DJ Thank you all for such a delightful evening!

Pete Oi! Your Earlship, any chance of a reward?

DJ A cheque is in the post! Goodnight, sweet ladies, goodnight!

He grabs Stan and they bomb for the exit, leaving the wailing, gnashing, gibbering chaos behind.

Act Three

Soho Square. Two in the morning.
    A Statue of King Charles II, face dimly lit.
    A Vagabond asleep on the ground beneath an old blanket.
    DJ on a bench, enjoying a bag of chips and swigging from a can of Pepsi. Stan is pacing, angrily.

Stan Sardanapalus!

DJ Ah.

Stan Did a project on him at school.

DJ Legendary Assyrian king, identity subject to considerable speculation.

Stan That's the feller! Reputed to be the biggest perv in ancient history. He used to tart around in ladywear, loved having his face rubbed with pumice. Had a thing – I kid you not – for combing strands of purple twine. No one quite knows *why*. On a whim, burnt his palace down killing all his slaves, eunuchs, concubines, entire family and himself. Delacroix painted his death: Sardanapalus sits there gloating over a carnival of suffering, coolly admiring the orgy of destruction he's created. (*Beat.*) Question: do you believe in reincarnation?

DJ It's two in the morning, you're overwrought. Go home.

Stan We've got issues to discuss!

DJ I don't discuss 'issues' with *anyone*. It's a vile, infantile word and you'd be wise to eliminate it from your slim vocabulary.

Stan Don't you *care*?! A waitress *died* tonight, thrown overboard! And that groom, Adam – 'Ahoy there' – he's a goner, he's not waking up.

DJ It was an accident.

Stan But *you* caused it!

DJ Oh, don't be *naive*, the *lady* caused it. We saw the fox and were compelled to give chase.

Stan (*aside*) I can't handle this any more.

DJ Do you know the derivation of the word 'Soho'? It's rather good: it was a hunting cry. (*Imitates a hunter.*) So-ho! *So-ho!* In the seventeenth century this was all fields. A gentleman would hunt fox and deer, right here. *So-ho!*

Stan I've got an announcement: I resign. This is me resigning. I've resigned.

DJ (*pauses for effect*) Thanks for your service.

Stan Right, you're obviously mortified so I'll have my wages and then I'll be gone. We can nip over to your house, you'll sign a cheque – you owe me twenty-seven thousand and eleven pounds – and then you'll never see me again.

DJ As you wish. (*Beat.*) Mind if I finish my snack?

Stan 'As you wish.'

DJ contemplates a chip, holds it up, closes one eye.

DJ You are rendered invisible by a little, fat chip. Perspective. Isn't it odd?

He eats the chip.

What are you going to do instead? Hmm?

Stan I'll drive a minicab, I don't care. I want a quiet life: nice wife, kids, a little garden, the odd holiday . . .

Stan starts to well up with longing.

DJ Is that really what you want?

Stan Yes!

DJ It's death. What you describe is *death*.

Stan No, it's life! It's what *people do*. It's real life!

DJ It's not worth living.

Stan I want to live it! I *want* to live it! (*Passionately.*) I want to *live* it!

DJ eats some more chips, swigs, muses:

DJ Whatever happened to old Soho, eh? When I was fifteen a brass was a brass, not some scraggy, abducted prisoner. Walker's Court, Rupert Street, Jimmy's, Pollo, good ol' Charlie Chester's. A felt-tipped sign pinned in a dirty doorway: 'MODEL'. The most seductive lie in the language. I remember. (*Faux cockney.*) ''Ere, son, get us twenty Rothmans and I'll give you a gobble.' 'Alright, but don't forget to take your teeth out.' 'Cheeky pup!' (*Sighs.*) God, I remember when cappuccino was a *delicacy*. You'd hang at the Bar Italia and slurp your continental coffee and score some hash and ogle the girls and you were a *prince*. Twenty years ago I could get stoned, blown and a cab home and still have change from a tenner. (*Wistfully.*) Where did it all *go*?

Want a chip?

Stan shakes his head.

Oh, go on, I know your little belly, you're always nibbling on something.

Stan takes a chip. And another. And another.

Have the bag, old chum.

Stan Thanks.

Stan sits down and feasts, ravenous.

DJ Condiment?

Stan adds salt from a sachet DJ hands him. DJ watches him, amused.

Swig of Pepsi-Cola?

Stan nods, gulps it down. DJ takes his drugs tin out.

Dab of MD?

Stan thinks, then shakes his head.

Spot of crack? Hunk of skunk? It's top drawer, blow your head off . . .

Stan Ooh, I wouldn't say no to a joint.

DJ There we go, you're perking up already! So let's have no more of this 'resignation' nonsense.

Stan I'm still leaving!

DJ Oh, you just need to get laid.

Stan It's not all about sex!

DJ Well, you say that . . .

Stan Tell you what I think . . . can I?

DJ nods.

Because your mother passed away when you were young you don't trust women, you expect them to reject you so the more you have the more –

DJ You're boring me! Stop it!

Stan You fear being alone, you can't be alone, you're *never* alone. That's the truth.

DJ Very shrewd.

Stan (*loftily*) Just discussing the *issues*.

DJ But wrong. There are no dark crannies here. No hidden corners for the tiddly torch of your analysis to illuminate. I *know* what I am and I understand it: I'm a child, a creature only of want. I choose this life and I own it. And no one owns *me*. Free will: it's the only thing we all have. And the only thing worth having. And most of us deny we have it at all. Now, we need some Rizlas. Ask if he's got some, they usually do.

He points to the sleeping Vagabond.

Stan He's in his kip.

DJ No askee, no spliffy.

Stan approaches the Vagabond and gently wakes him. The Vagabond stirs.

Stan Very sorry to disturb you but I don't s'pose you've got a Rizla? (*Mimes extensively.*) *Rizla?*

The Vagabond hands him some.

Cheers, mate.

DJ hands his tin to Stan who starts rolling a joint. DJ nods his thanks to the Vagabond who is now fully awake.

DJ Thank you for your generosity. Damn good of you.

Pause.

Vagabond May it please Allah.

DJ and Stan slowly turn to the Vagabond.

DJ I beg your pardon?

Vagabond May it please Allah.

DJ I must warn you that your Rizla will be used to consume the weed of the Infidel. I don't know if your God would approve . . . ?

Vagabond Allah is merciful.

DJ Thank Christ for that.

Stan senses trouble . . .

Vagabond And if you were to make a small donation he would be most grateful.

DJ Would he now. (*Sighs.*) Is nothing freely given in this world?

Vagabond Just a small contribution.

DJ Tell you what, I'll give you my watch. It's worth six grand.

He takes it off and dangles it before the Vagabond.

You may examine the goods.

The Vagabond does so. Then he reaches for the watch but DJ whips it away.

Uh-uh! (*Pause.*) You can have it . . . if you blaspheme against Allah.

Vagabond I don't understand.

DJ I will give you this watch if you insult your God. After all, what's he ever done for you, eh?

Vagabond He is in my soul. He protects me. I praise him. Always.

DJ You're a beggar! You've got nothing. You *smell*. What the fuck has Allah done for *you*?

Stan (*to DJ*) Please don't.

DJ (*to Stan*) We must be *realistic* about these things, it's the *bullshit* I can't stand.

He dangles the watch before the Vagabond.

You'll get a grand from any pawnbroker in town.

The Vagabond stares at the watch. Wants it.

Now *please*, I'd be delighted to give it to you. It's very special – a wedding gift from my wife. Look, the inscription: 'My heart, my soul, forever.' You see? Now we both know you want it. So just one teeny, little blaspheme and it's yours. Say . . . 'Allah has crapped on me.'

Vagabond No.

DJ But he *has*, it's *true*.

Vagabond Allah is merciful.

Pause.

DJ Call him a cunt.

Stan (*aside*) You see, just when you're beginning to warm to the man.

DJ Alright. If that's too harsh, call him a silly sausage.

Vagabond I will not insult him.

DJ Call him a twerp. For a thousand pounds . . .

Pause.

Vagabond I will not blaspheme.

They stare at each other. A long time. Finally:

DJ (*casually*) Then have it.

DJ gives the Vagabond the watch. He quickly slips it into his pocket and goes on his way.

Stan Was that really necessary?

DJ Who are *you*? You're just some *bloke*. Once you're back on the payroll you can do your disapproving.

Stan You could've given *me* that watch!

DJ Why? He deserved it, for his *integrity*. Are you as loyal as he?

Suddenly – loud noises offstage.

Male Voice (*off*) Help! Help!

They look offstage. See a fight.

DJ A fight! Three against one. That's not fair! WHO WANTS SOME!

He runs off.

(*Off.*) Good evening, gentlemen. Would you care for some violence?

The fight continues. Dreadful sounds of fists flying. Screams of pain.
Stan watches in horror. Lights his joint to calm himself down. Which it does.
Eventually, sounds of men running away.
DJ re-enters, dragging a heavily bloodied young man with him.
They fall to the ground, exhausted. DJ kneels, cradles the young man who is still in shock.

Young Man Thank you. Thank you!

DJ wipes his blood off.

DJ Good Lord, it's Col!

Col (*seeing DJ*) Oh, God! *You!*

Aloysius (*off*) Col! Col!

Col Here! I'm here!

Aloysius runs on. A fit, tough man of around thirty. He sees his younger brother, the blood and DJ.

Aloysius What's he done to you?

Col Nothing! He saved me!

Aloysius Never!

Aloysius squares up to DJ, who is ready to take him on, exhilarated by the prospect.

Col I was being mugged, he came to my rescue!

Aloysius (*to DJ*) Did you?

DJ Good evening, Vicious Aloysius. It's true, I am his saviour. Though not intentionally. Please, feel free to proceed. But I warn you, I have the advantage: unlike you I'm not afraid to die. And I fight dirty. So think on, you big nob.

A howl of pain from Col and Aloysius rushes to him.

(*To Stan.*) And where were *you*, trusted Tonto, while I was in jeopardy? (*Sees the lit joint.*) Ah ha!

Stan shrinks in shame. Aloysius is now attending to Col's wounds.

Aloysius Are you OK? D'you need an ambulance?

Col I'll be alright. (*Grunts in pain.*) I lost you, sorry.

Aloysius Don't speak, just breathe. That's it. That's it.

DJ I do have basic first aid, am available to administer kiss of life.

Aloysius Shut it.

DJ You have a cute little ass by the way. Very pert for a gent.

Aloysius springs up.

43

Aloysius Don't push it. I will gut you like a fish.

DJ Is this how you treat *family*? I'm still your brother-in-law.

Aloysius My little sister is suicidal. YOU ARE NOT FAMILY!

DJ Well, it's a moot point.

Aloysius goes back to Col. DJ saunters back to Stan and they sit on a bench, sharing the joint.

Aloysius You OK? Cos I'm gonna do it now. He's here, I'll have him.

Col You can't! Not now, not *tonight*. He saved my life, they could've killed me.

Aloysius One unintended favour is not equivalent to the hurt he caused Elvira.

Col I know but –

Aloysius No 'buts', *now*!

Col I cannot condone it, we must be *together* in this action. We must be *better* than him. He has done a good deed, in return we must offer him the opportunity to repent.

Aloysius What?!

Col We *must* give him the chance to make amends. Elvira still loves him. For whom do we act here?

Aloysius And suppose there is no other opportunity such as this?

Col There will be. We know his house. We know his moves. And the sidekick is biddable. He loathes him, would welcome the justice we'll exact upon him.

On the bench Stan and DJ are getting a little giggly together.

Aloysius I want him to go to hell.

Col And he *will*. I swear it. *If* he fails to take this opportunity.

DJ (*to Stan*) How about a little sortie down Dean Street? Let's find some company, eh?

Stan What, like some *female* company?

DJ Gosh, I hadn't *thought* of that! You wicked little gnome!

Stan chortles. DJ gives him an affectionate cuddle. Aloysius has helped Col to his feet. They face DJ and Stan.

Col Thank you.

DJ Any time.

Col I appreciate what you just did. But now I ask you to appreciate *our* situation. Our sister is dying of a broken heart. You broke it, will you now repair it? Will you go to her and swear to be a loyal and faithful husband from this moment on?

DJ One does hate to quibble but she really *isn't* dying of a broken heart. Her heart is an organ and *yes*, I played it and *yes*, she's upset. It was a rotten thing to do and I am a rotter. (*Salaciously.*) But she had some not inconsiderable *fun* and felt herself loved and in a manner of speaking she *was*. No. I will not go and 'repair her broken heart'.

He does a mocking little jig.

Aloysius (*to Col*) Satisfied?

Col nods, stunned. Aloysius approaches DJ. They face each other, close, intense. Aloysius draws out a knife from his pocket. The blade is sharp.

Aloysius We will meet again. Be assured of it.

DJ Whenever you want.

Aloysius Until then.

Col and Aloysius start to leave. Stan calls out:

Stan Ya shitters!

*Aloysius turns back furiously but Col pulls him away.
They exit.*
DJ and Stan sit there, smoking.

DJ You may be a disloyal little runt but you roll an
absolute ripper of a joint.

DJ rubs a wound, winces a touch.

Stan (*worried*) You OK?

DJ Mmm. Would you like to log that Lottie? On your
darling, little database.

Stan But you said I couldn't.

DJ We've both said a lot of things. Kiss and make up?

Stan thinks.

Pretty please? With a big, red cherry on top?

Stan Oh . . . alright!

They hug.

DJ You see? We can't be parted, we're joined at the
groin! A runt and a cunt!

Stan To be in your orbit, it's *so* . . .?

DJ Intoxicating.

He looks up, enraptured.

Look at the stars. You don't often see them in town.

They both gaze upwards.

Stan In the country you do. The night sky used to terrify me. It's so *huge*.

DJ opens his arms.

DJ I love this city. I love all cities. I'm in love with everyone and everything.

A moment of rapture. Gently, over the air, the sweet, gentle tune of 'Under a Blanket of Blue' drifts in. They sing a duet and slow dance in each other's arms. The company might provide choral accompaniment.

They gaze at each other for a while.
 Then DJ thinks, turns away from Stan and stares out front, distantly, sadly.
 And now he makes his invitation . . .

DJ Ask him if he wants to come down Dean Street.

Stan Who?

DJ doesn't look behind him. But knows.

DJ Him.

Stan What, *him*?!

Stan points to the Statue but DJ doesn't look at it.

DJ He needs cheering up. All alone, every night for centuries. Pigeons using his face as a khazi. Ask him along.

Stan Done!

Stan gets up, wanders over to the Statue. Weaving, light on his feet, stoned.

Your Royal Highness, sir. Me and . . . and my, my *master* are going down Dean Street. Maybe take in a show of the nudie variety, maybe get lucky, procure some . . . some . . .

ladies. We were wondering if you fancy coming? On us. An adventure. What d'you say?

Silence. Stan doesn't see the Statue open its eyes.

(*To Statue*.) Come on, mate. Get off your pedestal, come and have some fun!

A terrible sound of grinding stone and the Statue faces Stan.

Statue No.

Stan (*terrified*) Hrrr – hhhh – rrrr – hhhh – help!

DJ What?

Stan (*pointing*) S-ssssstatue spoke.

DJ You're stoned!

Stan is rooted to the spot – frozen like a statue pointing at the Statue.

Stan Hurrr – haaaa – he sssspeak. He speak. He's shpoekerrrnnnn. A wuuuurrdd!

DJ Rubbish!

DJ staggers over. He tries to unfreeze Stan but it's impossible. Stan is in spasm.

(*To Statue*.) Did you speak?

Statue Yes.

DJ He spoke! He spoke! He bloody SPOKE!

Now DJ is rooted to the spot, gibbering with fear, pointing like Stan.

Stan I know!

DJ We're imagining it!

Stan We can't *both* be!

DJ We must be!

Stan Run for it!

DJ Can't move!

Stan Me neither!

Pause.

DJ (*to Statue*) What are you?

Statue Recognition.

Pause.

DJ Are you alive?

Statue I come from the dead.

Pause.

DJ Why?

Statue You know why. You have always known.

Pause.

DJ To take me?

Statue Yes.

DJ When?

Statue TOMORROW!

Stan exits, screaming. DJ stares at the Statue.

Act Four

Six in the morning. DJ's House in Meard Street, Soho.
The main room.

Dalia lies on a chaise longue. She reaches over to the
small coffee table, dabs her finger in what's left of the
coke, lines her gums with it. Kristal enters from the
bedroom followed soon after by Ruby. 'Three Graces'.
All half dressed and post-coital.

They loll about. Tired. One of them fiddles with a
remote control. Presses a button. Loud music snaps on.
They vaguely move to it, listlessly.

After a while DJ bounces in from his bedroom. He
wears a silk dressing gown and velvet slippers with
elaborate gold brocade initials: 'DJ'. The hookers snap
into action and dance about.

DJ poses – deliriously. Opens his dressing gown to
reveal he's wearing women's knickers. The hookers react
with delight. Now he starts dirty dancing with the women.
They bump and grind, having a ball.

The mini-orgy continues as the door buzzer sounds.
They can't hear it. But we can – just.

After a while, Stan emerges from another bedroom in
faded boxer shorts, a scraggy T-shirt and one charcoal
grey sock. He watches the oblivious dancers, consumed
with envy. The buzzer keeps sounding.

Stan stomps over to the intercom phone on the wall and
picks up. He shouts like a maniac to make himself heard.
He listens. And then smiles as he gleans who's there. He
buzzes them in. Then he puts the receiver back on the
hook and plucks the remote control from the arm of the
sofa. He presses a button and the music stops instantly.

Stan Your father's here.

DJ Don't let him in!

Stan He's in already. The Earl is in the building. He's having a jimmy riddle downstairs. You've got about forty-five seconds. Any requests?

DJ (*points at coffee table*) *This!*

Stan Good call.

Stan exits.

Dalia Mister, do you want for us to go fuck off?

She speaks with an unidentifiable East European accent.

DJ Most certainly not. You are my honoured guests. Sit.

They curl up on the sofa. DJ hands them a bottle of whisky.

Ruby I like this drink. Thank you, Mister Donwan.

The girls share swigs from the bottle, licking drops from each other's lips.

DJ Oh, you delicious slatterns.

Sound of loo flushing downstairs.

STANLEY!

Stan appears in a pinny, with a feather duster on a long stick.

Stan Would sir care for me to titivate the room?

DJ Yes! Yes! Yes!

Stan intentionally and pointlessly flutters his duster in a high crevice.

Do the bloody *table*!

Stan Oh, silly me, I clean forgot!

He very slowly picks a fag end out of an ashtray on the table and pops it in a bin liner.

Louis (*off*) I'm coming up!

DJ (*to Stan*) DO IT!

Stan 'As you wish.'

DJ Do it now or I will thrash you!

Stan places the bin liner over the whole table, picks it up and exits with the table concealed within the bag. Dalia, Ruby and Kristal applaud.
DJ straightens his robe and sets himself in a pose of elaborate respectability to receive his father; hands clasped in his middle, feet at ninety degrees.
The hookers follow suit, assuming appropriate positions to receive a member of the aristocracy.
Footsteps approach up the stairs. DJ is completely still. Waiting. Tense.

Dalia You have cocaine on your chinny chin.

DJ (*wipes it off*) Thank you.

Louis comes in. A man in his seventies. He surveys the scene with contempt.

Good evening, Father.

Louis It's six o'clock in the morning. I have journeyed five hours through black, murderous night. The chauffeur has a fucking hernia. I drove myself, assaulted each mile by hail and spiteful sleet. I am shattered. I want coffee.

From nowhere DJ produces a little bell which he tinkles. Stan appears.

Stan (*to Louis*) Good morning, My Lord.

DJ My father would like some coffee.

Stan (*to Louis*) I remember; strong and black, one sugar?

Louis Thank you . . . er . . . ?

Stan Stan.

Louis Why the hell are you wearing a pinny?

Stan To conceal my underwear from your gaze, sir.

DJ Ladies, would you care for some coffee?

Dalia Do you hef a cepoocheeno?

Ruby and Kristal nod in agreement.

Louis (*to Stan*) Don't bother, the harlots will be leaving. I shall talk to my son in private.

DJ (*to Stan*) Make them their coffees.

Louis (*to DJ*) Send your painted ladies away!

DJ (*angrily*) You stand in my house, you do not speak ill of my friends!

Louis (*furiously*) Feed them their cash and rid this room of them!

DJ No!

They glare at each other.

Stan (*aside*) This is actually quite *civil*. They've not spoken in three years.

Louis stares at his son. Thinks. Concedes.

Louis Very well.

DJ nods. Stan exits to make coffee. Silence.

DJ (*to Louis*) Would you like to sit down?

He gestures to the sofa. The hookers make a little space for Louis.

Louis I'll stand.

DJ What's on your mind, Pops?

Louis Elvira's father has communicated the news. I wish I were shocked but nothing you do surprises me. Aged seven I found you masturbating your sister's pony, the rest has been inevitable.

DJ I was *curious*, name a small boy who isn't.

Louis To the matter. Your wife. Is there any hope of a rapprochement?

DJ No.

Louis Look, I do understand the bloody itch. I wasn't a monk myself. But you're not young any more. It's undignified. You simply can't, you just can't continue to live for pleasure alone. Why not? Aside from the decadent selfishness of it all you have *responsibilities*. We employ more than three hundred people on the estate. Good, decent people who depend on us and we on them. And when I'm dead they will depend on *you*. It's a *community*. And yes, I loathe the word too but dammit, it *is*. Your boy – (*Gestures to the kitchen.*) I remember his great-grandfather. *He* doesn't. (*Beat.*) Continuity. Belonging. Family. Home. Why do you so despise these things? Why are simple human values so abhorrent to you? What strange path presented itself to you? When? Was it my fault? If so, *tell* me. Hmm? I'm not asking you to – to go to bloody church. *I* like a drink. I like a cigar. (*Nods to the hookers.*) I look at these women and weep for what I was. To have a woman – women like this – these *beauties* – I'd have to pay through the nose. But you *choose* to! *Why*? You demean yourself and them. What's so wrong with being good? Good is *good*. It just is. And God knows, *I'm* no bloody good. But *you* – you've never done an honest day's work in your life! I mean literally. You have

54

ponced and preened and primped your way through – all funded by idiot me and the judicious industry of your ancestors. You stand to inherit a fortune. Don't force me to cut you off. I will do it, sonny, I will change my will, I wouldn't want to but I would, I'll give it all to your siblings if you don't buck up! Honour! It must be in you *somewhere*? It's in *everyone*, even the lowest common thief knows his place in the moral landscape. Does any of this make any sense at all? Sorry, I'm so terribly tired. Elvira is jolly and nice and so dedicated to you. And to 'people' in general. (*Beginning to weep.*) An angel! Why cause her such appalling sorrow? I'm so ashamed of you . . . and so ashamed to be so disappointed in my own boy . . .

He holds his head, in deep sadness.

Dalia (*to DJ*) If you want us to do sex with him we hef to make price cos it's extra.

DJ That won't be necessary. He's going now. Fuck off, Dad. See you in another three years.

Silence. Louis can't move. Stan comes in with a tray of coffees. Beautiful china. He serves Louis first then the others. Louis drinks his coffee in a few gulps while everyone watches.

Louis Thank you, Stan.

Ruffles Stan's hair.

That was an excellent cup of coffee.

Stan Will you be staying at your flat or the club?

Louis Erm . . . the club. (*To hookers.*) I apologise for my atrocious manners when I arrived. Unforgivable.

The ladies shrug, unconcerned.

(*To DJ.*) Goodnight.

Stan I'll see you out.

Stan and Louis exit.

Ruby Your dad: he's a sweetie.

DJ Listen, fuckface, *you're* the sweetie. To the bedroom! (*Hunting cry.*) So-ho!

The hookers get up and scamper off to his room.
DJ is alone on stage, for the first time.
He stands in the room. Completely still. Silence. It is as if he has ceased to exist.
Footsteps up the stairs. Stan comes back in. DJ is alive again.
Stan starts tidying up the coffee cups, won't look at DJ.

Oh, don't be so pissy! (*Pause.*) OK. *Yes.* Last night I said we'd *share* but when it came to it I wanted them for myself. *Sorry.* But you have whims and I have needs. (*Sighs.*) You may take one of them to the box room. The short one.

Stan I'm not angry about that. I was but I'm over it.

DJ Good, all the more puss for me.

He starts to exit towards his bedroom.

Stan (*furiously*) You just don't get it! Your father drove *five hours*! And now he's sobbing in the street!

DJ Three almost criminally gifted tarts are waiting to anoint my phallus, do you think I care?

Stan I know you don't! It's just I had *hopes*! Last night, there was genuine compassion in you!

DJ And it was real. And so is this.

He makes to exit.

Stan And the *statue*? Aren't you worried about that? Cos I can't *sleep*!

Pause.

DJ It was a hallucination.

Suddenly – loud footsteps coming up the stairs.

Stan (*scared*) Who's that??

They listen in fear as the footsteps approach. And then, Elvira comes in, holding her keys. They stare at her.

Elvira I've come for my clothes.

She tosses DJ her keys and heads for the bedroom.

DJ Ah, I wouldn't go in there just yet.

Elvira I'll go wherever I want.

Dalia (*off*) Oh, Mr Donwan!

Elvira (*halts*) Who's that?

Dalia (*off*) Oh, dirty Mr Donwan!

DJ It's the new cleaner.

Ruby (*off*) Mister Donwan! We are *waiting*!

Elvira So who's *that*?

DJ The *old* cleaner.

Elvira Huh?

Stan The old cleaner's showing the new one what to do.

DJ (*to Stan, sotto*) Brilliant!

Dalia (*off*) Mister Donwan, are you gonna come and get fucked?

Ruby (*off*) And sucked and fucked again, Mr Donwan?

Kristal (*off*) And have smack in arse and punch on face?

Laughter off. Elvira stares at DJ.

Elvira Are they *prostitutes*?

DJ I believe remuneration has been discussed but it's Stan's bailiwick.

Stan (*to Elvira*) Would you like some breakfast? I could nip down to Maison Bertaux, get you an eclair . . . ?

Elvira No, thank you.

Stan Well, I'll leave you to it. (*To DJ.*) . . . May I . . . ?

He indicates the bedroom thus to claim 'the short one'. DJ grants permission:

DJ Go. Guzzle.

Stan starts to exit.

Elvira No! I want *you* to hear this too!

Stan stops.

Stan (*aside*) Will this dreadful day never end?!

Elvira Don't be alarmed, I won't detain you long. Nor will I embarrass you with hysterical fits of emotion. I am cleansed. You have burnished me. I loved you. I still love you and always will. You gave me a great gift, you opened me up to physical pleasure, I believe you to be a true poet of the flesh. You made my soul sing. You made me believe I had found my eternal best friend. You were so kind and humorous and sweet. I know it was all lies, I know your dark purpose, but I refuse to hate you for it. Though I beg of you, *please* do not do to others as you have done to me. The pain is of an intensity I would not wish upon any living creature.

DJ (*to Stan, sotto*) Are you crying?

Stan (*sniffs*) Sorry.

DJ Stop it.

Elvira I know you have no belief in God. You scorn him. I think you are a nihilist posing as a libertine. But I will pray for you – and I urge you to think deeply about your life and resolve to live a better one. A just one. A life that embraces *light*. What terrible darkness you must inhabit to be so morally barren. It saddens me to think of the anguish that lives within you. The pain you must carry. How do you bear it? My fear is that something dreadful awaits you, that 'horror' will seek you out. I sense you have loaded the revolver . . . long, long ago . . . and you cannot perceive how hypnotised you are by the thrill of its deadliness. You are entranced by sensation – you share this sickness with the society that spawned you. But there is a great and glorious beauty in this world, the potential of what we might become. Please, please awaken yourself to it. With tears in my eyes – damn them – I beg you to repent. Save yourself, before it's too late!

She starts to exit.

Stan What about your clothes?

Elvira Give them to charity. Not another second in this house, my soul will perish.

She exits. DJ stares at the exit, seemingly in deep thought. But he is not.

DJ The saucy minx! Her dishevelment, her *passion*, that rambling, studenty splurge. Had she prepared it or was it 'impro'? (*Mock grandiose.*) She has stoked the embers of a fire I had long thought extinguished. (*Darkly.*) I'm gonna get her back.

Stan So none of it affected you?

DJ Not a syllable.

*Suddenly – incredibly loud, terrified screams from the
bedroom – Dalia, Kristal and Ruby come sprinting out,
clutching their clothes. They run across the room, still
screaming as they exit down the stairs. The front door
slams. Stan and DJ look at each other. Very scared.*

Pop into the bedroom will you, see what's what?

Stan Your bedroom. Your problem.

*DJ takes a few tentative steps towards the room and
then stops. Absolutely terrified. Stan has seen it too.
Once more he is frozen, his arm raised, pointing at . . .
the thing.*
*The Statue enters. Slowly. It is not human. Nor is it
made of stone. It is as if the statue they saw in Soho
Square has come to life. It is a dirty white, with mildew
and pigeon droppings on it. It moves naturally. Though
it speaks sonorously. It is the same age as DJ and might
even resemble him a little. It is both hideous and
beautiful.*

DJ Is it time?

The Statue stares at him.

Statue Tonight.

Pause.

DJ How will I die?

Statue The details are not yet determined.

DJ Is it avoidable?

Statue Use your time wisely.

*The Statue moves to exit. Stan and DJ watch it,
spellbound. The statue exits. Invisibly. Magically.
Ideally through a mirror. There are no footsteps down
the stairs. No sound of a front door closing. Stan
checks.*

Stan He's vanished.

Silence.

DJ Well, it's all a bit rum, isn't it?

Stan Just a bit. Do you believe it?

DJ Well, I don't know . . .

Stan It's just . . . if it *is* true I'm thinking you might want to get things in order . . . your papers and . . . *things.*

DJ I have no papers. (*Flatly.*) Oh. Your *wages.*

Stan You wouldn't want it on your conscience, would you?

DJ No. I'd hate to face extinction having failed to bung you your wedge.

But he does nothing, just stands there.

Stan Hate to nudge, take ten seconds to do it now . . .? You did *promise.*

DJ Every second is precious. I need to sleep. I'll attend to it when I wake. Do try to rise above yourself.

He exits. Stan starts tidying up. DJ re-enters.

This will be the first time I've slept alone . . . for as long as I can remember. (*Pause.*) I don't suppose . . .?

He looks almost pleadingly at Stan but it's clear that Stan won't.

Never mind.

He exits. Stan turns to the audience and tinkles the little bell in a melancholy fashion.

Act Five

A gentlemen's club. The morning room. 7.30 p.m. Later the same day.

Louis is sitting in an armchair. He is resplendent in a dinner jacket and black bow tie. On a little table in front of him, a half drunk glass of beer and his own malt whisky. Also, a silver tray containing nuts and olives.

Louis waits. Glowering. Crunching nuts.

Stan comes in, wearing an old suit and a scraggy tie.

Louis Where *is* the little shit?

Stan The porter says there's still no sign of him. I called his mobile, nothing.

He sits in an armchair, resumes drinking his beer.

Louis Help yourself to an olive. Or nut.

Stan Oh, thanks very much.

Stan takes an olive, briskly shakes the oil off, carefully inserts a single nut inside it and then pops the lot in his mouth. Louis watches this, disgusted.

Louis What did you say he wants?

Stan He phoned me this evening, around six, said he'd just woken up and he *had* to see you. Wanted me here too. Wouldn't say why or what, just that it was incredibly important.

Louis I will not tolerate another vowel of his abuse.

Stan Tell me about it.

Louis What?

Stan I said, 'Tell me about it.'

Louis *What?*

Stan I mean, 'me neither', on the abuse front.

Louis (*abusively*) What are you fucking talking about?

Stan The *abuse*, *I* won't tolerate another vowel of it. Like *you*.

Louis Damn right! Yes! Don't take it from anyone! Just because you're a servant it doesn't give your betters the right to take the piss. This club, see the staff? All the staff, running around, what are they?

Stan . . . People . . . ?

Louis Of course they are! But what *are* they?

Stan . . . I don't know.

Louis *Happy!* They are happy people! Why? Because they are not abused. This club is a self-supporting system of mutual respect. We respect them, they respect us, bob's your uncle. Where *is* the suppurating pustule? I'm supposed to be at a function.

Stan Is it nearby, I could call you a taxi . . . ?

Louis It's downstairs, you tit.

They sit in silence for a while.
DJ enters. Immaculate. His hair is tidy, his suit exquisite. His tie has a perfect Windsor knot. A silk handkerchief is folded in a neat triangle in his top pocket.

DJ My sincere apologies for keeping you waiting. May I?

Louis nods and DJ sits in Stan's chair. Pause.

Louis Drink?

DJ I won't, thank you.

Stan is flabbergasted.

Stan (*aside*) He's not refused a drink for ten years.

Louis Well?

DJ I slept badly so please forgive me if this comes out in something of a ramble. I don't mean that as an excuse. I mean it's difficult to find the adequate words to express the magnitude of my apology. (*Pause.*) Dad, and Stan, I'm sorry. I'm sorry for subjecting you both to so many *years* of pain and torment. And I want you both to know how grateful I am that you're still here. It means the world to me. Much more than I deserve. (*Pause.*) I'm so appalled by what I've done to Elvira. And I want to make amends if I can. I will see her next. I want her to know how much I regret hurting her. And I want to thank her for seeing me earlier today and for her concern, her deep concern about the way I have lived. And the poor girl knows only a fraction of it. You, Stan, know the worst. You know me better than anyone on earth and yet . . . here you are. Good old Stan. (*Starts to cry.*) Sorry. Sorry.

Stan squeezes his hand.

Louis Have a drink. Let me order you a drink.

DJ No, please, Dad. I really mustn't. That's all part of it. The drink, the drugs, the sex. The whole pattern. I want to *change*. I feel as though I've been living another life, someone else's life, the life of someone I now fear.

He wipes some tears away with his handkerchief.

(*To Louis.*) You gave me this. On my twenty-first.

Louis nods, remembering.

I – I need help – can't do it on my own. Too weak. But there are . . . places, clinics. And . . . I don't know how long I've got. I sense my time has run out. (*Softly.*) I don't want to die.

Louis But you won't. You're in remarkably good health given your . . . habits.

DJ I want to go *home*. I – I want to visit Mum's grave. I need to talk to her. I can't bear it that she died knowing how dissolute I was. I can't make her proud. But I will make *you* proud, Dad. I swear it. And you, Stan, I'll make it all up to you.

Louis You *do* make me proud. I *am* proud. Come here!

DJ falls into his father's arms, sobbing his heart out.

Do you hear me? I'm proud of you. This took guts. My God, you've got guts.

Stan joins the weeping little huddle. It becomes a three-way man hug.

Stan Well done, well done!

Louis Look, I'm supposed to be at this bloody function but sod it, let's all have dinner!

DJ *No*, thank you, I need to see Elvira, as soon as I can. And apologise to her brothers too. But perhaps we could have breakfast tomorrow?

Louis Yes. Oh, yes! *Breakfast.*

They continue to hug a little longer.

DJ Thank you so much for seeing me. For being here.

Louis (*overwhelmed*) My pleasure. Goodnight, son. Goodnight, Stan. Bloody well done!

He exits. Stan gazes at DJ.

Stan Good on you.

DJ smiles. He was knotting the handkerchief at each corner throughout his 'apology' and now places it on his head as if it were a hat.

NOOOOOHHHHH!

DJ plucks a hip flask from his jacket pocket, takes a big slug of scotch.

DJ I have been strangely fuckless for more than twelve hours! Onwards now, to *So-ho*!

The scene changes. DJ and Stan are now on the street outside Louis's club. DJ starts looking for a taxi.

Taxi!

Stan But WHY?!

DJ Cos Daddy's got the dough! If he cuts me off I'd have to get a *job* – like every other miserable drudge on this planet! You really bought that crap about Mummy's grave? I thought I was pushing it there?

Stan I was MOVED!

DJ Well don't be moved by me. *Ever.*

Stan (*mournfully*) Why did I believe?

DJ Because you wanted to! (*Shadow boxes a bit, bobbing, weaving.*) I feel *frisky*, getting it up for all that bullshit sincerity has given me the horn!

Stan What about the statue? It pronounced your *death*!

DJ A stunt – smoke and mirrors – 'weird shit'! I'm far too alive to die, I just needed some sleep! Tonight, I shall seduce the moon, the stars and everything that moves beneath the trembling sky. So-ho!

Stan I CAN'T BEAR IT!

DJ Oh, it won't be like this *for ever*. Another twenty or thirty years and we'll retire to the country – promise. A yokel a day will suffice in my dotage.

Stan What about 'good old Stan', who 'knows me better than anyone on earth'? Was that bit true? You made me feel so *needed*.

DJ Well you are, you're my accomplice.

Stan Is that *all*?

DJ I'm fond of you, what more d'you want?

Stan (*passionately*) I want to be loved! I thought you LOVED me! I thought I was *special*!

Pause.

DJ Are you coming or what?

Stan No.

Stan looks away, brooding, deeply disappointed.

DJ (*gently, at first*) I won't pretend to love you when I don't. The honesty is a compliment. You're the only person I don't lie to. We live in an age of apology, don't confuse it with authenticity. At least my lies are honest – at least I know *when* I'm lying and *why*. Would you prefer me to be a hypocrite? It's easily done and terribly vogue – look around you; hypocrisy is both vice *and* virtue – it doesn't even shock us. The bankers rob banks, the police are criminals and politicians have no politics. Governments don't govern, newspapers invent news, peace-preaching rulers wage war. It's *everywhere*! Holy writ perverted to murder, billionaire tax dodgers, pension fund plunderers, racists posing as patriots, judges with no judgement, priests who prey (with an 'e'). Global poverty, insane famine, a planet burning itself to hell – and the most powerful man upon it? A charlatan, a fake tan, an orang-utan! And the people? Corrupted, broken-hearted, clinging to whatever floats a boat in this ocean of injustice: every second sucker with a story to sell – memoirs, confessions, outpourings – a deluge of diaries for a world of professional weepers. Family histories – ooh, my ancestry – here's a gif of my first little poo. ME ME ME ME ME ME ME ME. You're a chef – cook – SHUT UP! You're a gardener – garden – SHUT UP! We pimp our precious lives to the infernal gnashing babble – Follow me! Friend me! Like me! But don't ever *know* me. Every tedious twot in Christendom vomiting opinion – LEAVE ME ALONE! BE QUIET! A million years ago – some hairy bastard daubed a horse on the wall of his cave, he saw it, he drew it – well done! Flash forward: 'Hello, welcome to my vlog. Today I bought a plum.' You *cunt*! You silly dozy twit, you've forgotten HOW TO LIVE! Whatever happened to privacy? To grace and decorum? *Elegance*? To life as we knew it? Hmm? Oh, dear sweet Stan, Darwin got it *wrong*; man didn't evolve, he just got nicer tools. From a lump of charcoal to the iPhone – whoosh – *history*. (*Softly, intensely.*) Where's the *poetry*, hmm? Where's the *soul*?

Stan I take your point, but you're not human.

DJ On the contrary, I am 'uberly' human. This is *homo sapiens* in his natural animal state, existing only in the present moment: TO HUNT. A good fuck is worth dying for – and if you don't know what I mean you've never had one. Aha! Transport! Here! Over here!

DJ waves and whistles. A cycle rickshaw comes on. The Statue is pedalling it.

Stan (*terrified*) STATUE!

Stan points, frozen again. DJ stares at the statue. Thinks. Then:

DJ So how long have I got? (*Pause.*) Oi, Chalky, how long?

The statue is silent. DJ approaches it, his fear subsiding. He gets up close and faces the statue. A long look.

I defy you.

He climbs aboard the rickshaw. Somewhere there is music, 'The Thrill of It All' by Roxy Music.

(*To Statue.*) Soho at the double! (*To Stan.*) You coming? Yes? No? Maybe?

Stan No.

They stare at each other, both recognising this is the end.

DJ Bye then.

Stan exits. DJ watches him go, impassively.

(*To Statue.*) So-ho!

As the music crashes in the Statue pedals away and the scene changes.
Sounds of Soho begin to rise. People, laughter, screams, cars, taxis, the thrilling ambience of the city at night . . .
A phantasmagorical soundscape – and the music within it and over it and under it.
DJ is exhilarated – a king returning to his kingdom. Flying.
He stands and salutes the streets – right and left – as they flash past, he blows kisses to them from his speeding chariot.

Hello, Great Windmill!
Evening, Archer!
Alright, Brewer!
Luscious Lexington!
Respect to little Beak!

(*Bows, gravely.*) Good evening, sombre Broadwick.
   Dean, Frith and Greek!
   How ya doing, old Poland?
   And plucky little D'Arblay!

(*To Statue*) OK, this'll do fine.

   But the Statue keeps pedalling.

I'll get off here, mate!

   But the Statue keeps pedalling.

Hey, I said stop, please!

   But the Statue keeps pedalling. DJ is scared now.

Where are we going?

   But the Statue keeps pedalling.

Hey! STOP!!!

   *The Statue stops. Abruptly. DJ is thrown to the
   ground. The sounds of Soho fade away.*
       *DJ looks around. It's silent now. The Statue
   remains. Watching him.*

Where are we? . . . No streets . . . no lights . . . where are
the people . . . ? Where are we . . . ?

Statue The place of your death.

   Pause.

DJ Why?

   The Statue seems momentarily confused.

Statue You summoned me.

DJ When?

Statue Last night. In the square. You invited me to join
you.

70

DJ I was not myself.

Statue You are always yourself. It is *that* you cannot bear.

DJ I don't believe in you. I *choose* not to believe in you!

Statue I *am* you.

They stare at each other. DJ understands now.

DJ Recognition.

The Statue pedals off.
It's dark. Very distant sounds of Soho. Seemingly miles away. DJ turns around. Peers. Turns again. Lost. There's nothing. He is nowhere.

What place is this . . . ? Where . . . where is the *life* . . .? Hello? . . . Hello . . .? . . . Soho . . .? Someone . . . ? Help!

Col and Aloysius appear. They wear gloves. DJ is grateful to see them.

Col. Aloysius. Thank God! I'm completely lost. Where the hell are we?

Pause.

Col We are alone.

DJ That's not a place.

Pause.

Aloysius Yes it is.

He draws his knife. DJ tries to run but they force him to the ground. Col kneels on his arms. Aloysius sits on DJ's legs. He struggles, desperately.

DJ HELP! HELP! HELP!

Aloysius takes the handkerchief from DJ's top pocket, hands it to Col, who stuffs it in DJ's mouth.

71

Aloysius Silence.

Muffled cries from DJ. Aloysius hits him across the face.

Listen to me. *Listen.*

DJ is silent.

You can save yourself. If you apologise – and convince us you mean it – then you won't die. We'll beat the hell out of you but we'll let you live. We want your apology: for what you did to our sister. For what you did to countless others. For how you live. For who you are.

Aloysius nods to Col who takes the gag out of DJ's mouth.

Well?

DJ No!

Aloysius Then you will die. (*To Col.*) Stop his mouth.

Col puts the gag back in DJ's mouth. Aloysius raises the knife.

A knife to your groin. Some pain for your pleasure.

Col (*to DJ*) He will do it, sir! Count on it. *Please*, spare yourself and apologise!

Aloysius is poised. He raises the knife again.

(*To Aloysius.*) Wait, he's trying to speak!

Col removes the gag.

Aloysius Well?

DJ No apology! *Never!*

Col You feel no guilt?

DJ None!

Aloysius No shame, no regret?

DJ None and none!

Col But it's *suicide*, don't you want to live?!

DJ YES! BUT ONLY AS I PLEASE!

Aloysius Gag him.

Col does so. DJ struggles. Col holds him down.

Now.

Aloysius plunges the knife into DJ's groin. He spasms, horribly. The knife – again. Col screams. The knife again. Aloysius screams. The knife: again. And again. The blood begins to flow.

And this for your cold selfish heart!

He stabs DJ in the heart. A spurt of blood.
  Aloysius withdraws the knife and he and Col run away, terrified.
  DJ writhes, screaming into the gag. He manages to remove it. Screams. Then, a pitiful cry. An agonised yelp of pure pain. A crawl on his belly. And then he slumps. A hideous gurgle. And he is dead.
  Gradually, a normal lighting state has emerged. Sounds of Soho.
  DJ is dead in Soho Square. The Statue on its plinth. The face dimly lit. Impassive.
  Stan enters. Sees the body. The blood. A gruesome sight.

Stan Mmm. Thought I'd find you here.

He peers at the body.

(*Quietly.*) Cold as an Eskimo.

Stan looks at the Statue a moment then turns to the audience . . .

73

The world is a better place without him. We will all sleep sweetly tonight. He is gone and everyone cheers. Except *me* – cos he never signed the cheque! I want my wages, my wages, my wages!

Stan exits.
DJ dead, alone.
The Statue, oblivious.
Sounds of the city at night.
Music travelling underneath.
Rising now.
The company enter and dance around the corpse.
Their feet splashing in the pool of blood.
Delirious joy as the living dance over the dead.
Climax.

End.